PATIENT SAFETY

AF448091

TABLE OF CONTENTS

INTRODUCTION

In the complex and ever-evolving field of healthcare, ensuring patient safety is paramount. The provision of safe, high-quality care is a fundamental responsibility of every healthcare provider, from doctors and nurses to administrators and support staff. "Patient Safety Essentials: A Comprehensive Guide for Healthcare Providers" is designed to be an informative and engaging resource, aimed at equipping healthcare professionals with the knowledge and skills necessary to prevent harm and improve patient outcomes.

Patient safety is a multifaceted concept that encompasses various aspects of healthcare delivery. It involves the prevention of errors, the reduction of risks, and the promotion of practices that lead to safe and effective patient care. The consequences of lapses in patient safety can be severe, ranging from minor injuries to life-threatening complications, and even death. As such, fostering a culture of safety within healthcare organizations is crucial.

By the end of this book, healthcare providers will have a comprehensive understanding of patient safety and the tools necessary to implement effective safety practices in their daily work. Whether you are a seasoned professional or new to the field, "Patient Safety Essentials: A Comprehensive Guide for Healthcare Providers" aims to be an invaluable resource in your commitment to providing safe, high-quality care.

MODULE ONE

LESSON ONE: PATIENT SAFETY

Patient safety is a critical aspect of healthcare that focuses on preventing and mitigating harm to patients during the provision of health services. This lesson lays the foundation for understanding the importance of patient safety, the history and evolution of patient safety practices, and the key concepts that underpin a culture of safety in healthcare.

The Importance of Patient Safety

Patient safety is essential for ensuring the well-being of patients and maintaining trust in the healthcare system. Harm to patients can result from errors, adverse events, and system failures. These incidents not only impact the health and lives of patients but also have significant financial and reputational consequences for healthcare organizations.

Historical Context

The concept of patient safety has evolved over time, with significant milestones shaping current practices. The publication of the Institute of Medicine's (IOM) report "To Err is Human: Building a Safer Health System" in 1999 was a pivotal moment that brought attention to the prevalence of medical errors and the need for systemic changes in healthcare. This report estimated that up to 98,000 deaths annually in the United States were due to preventable medical errors, highlighting the urgent need for improved safety measures.

Key Concepts in Patient Safety

Several key concepts are fundamental to understanding and promoting patient safety:

- Adverse Events: These are incidents that result in harm to a patient. Adverse events can be preventable or non-preventable and may occur due to errors, system failures, or complications of care.
- Near Misses: Also known as close calls, these are incidents that could have resulted in harm but did not, either by chance or timely intervention. Near misses are valuable learning opportunities for preventing future errors.
- System Approach: This perspective emphasizes that errors are often the result of system failures rather than individual negligence. By focusing on improving systems and processes, healthcare organizations can create safer environments for patients.
- Just Culture: A just culture promotes accountability and learning by distinguishing between human errors, at-risk behaviors, and reckless actions. It encourages reporting of errors and near misses without fear of punishment, fostering a culture of safety.

Building a Culture of Safety

Creating a culture of safety requires commitment and collaboration at all levels of a healthcare organization. Key elements of a culture of safety include:

- Leadership Commitment: Leaders play a crucial role in setting the tone for safety. They must prioritize patient safety, allocate resources, and support initiatives aimed at reducing harm.
- Teamwork and Communication: Effective teamwork and clear communication are vital for preventing errors and ensuring patient safety. Healthcare providers must work collaboratively, sharing information and coordinating care to avoid misunderstandings and mistakes.

- Continuous Improvement: A culture of safety is characterized by ongoing efforts to identify and address safety issues. This includes implementing evidence-based practices, conducting regular safety assessments, and learning from errors and near misses.

The Role of Healthcare Providers

Healthcare providers are at the forefront of patient safety efforts. They must be vigilant, knowledgeable, and proactive in preventing harm. This involves adhering to best practices, staying updated on safety guidelines, and participating in training and education programs.

Patient safety is a fundamental aspect of high-quality healthcare. By understanding its importance, embracing key concepts, and fostering a culture of safety, healthcare providers can significantly reduce the risk of harm to patients.

MODULE TWO

LESSON ONE: BUILDING A CULTURE OF SAFETY

A culture of safety is essential for minimizing risks and ensuring high-quality patient care. This lesson discusses the components of a culture of safety, the role of leadership, and strategies for fostering a safe healthcare environment.

The Importance of a Safety Culture

A safety culture is characterized by shared values, beliefs, and behaviors that prioritize safety above all else. In a strong safety culture, all members of the organization are committed to preventing harm and continuously improving safety. A positive safety culture leads to better patient outcomes, increased staff satisfaction, and reduced errors.

Components of a Culture of Safety

Key components of a culture of safety include:

- Leadership Commitment: Leaders must demonstrate a commitment to safety through their actions and decisions. This includes allocating resources, supporting safety initiatives, and setting clear expectations for safety.
- Teamwork and Collaboration: Effective teamwork and collaboration are vital for a safety culture. Healthcare providers must work together, communicate openly, and support one another in delivering safe care.
- Continuous Learning: A culture of safety promotes continuous learning and improvement. This involves

regular training, error reporting, and the implementation of evidence-based practices.

- Transparency and Accountability: Transparency in reporting errors and near misses is essential for learning and improvement. Accountability ensures that all members of the organization take responsibility for their actions and contribute to safety efforts.

The Role of Leadership

Leadership is a critical factor in building and sustaining a culture of safety. Leaders set the tone for the organization and influence its values and priorities. Key actions for leaders include:

- Setting a Vision: Leaders must articulate a clear vision for patient safety and communicate it effectively to all members of the organization.
- Modeling Behavior: Leaders should model safe behaviors and demonstrate a commitment to safety in their daily actions.
- Allocating Resources: Ensuring that adequate resources are available for safety initiatives, including staffing, training, and technology.
- Encouraging Reporting: Creating an environment where staff feel safe to report errors and near misses without fear of punishment.

Strategies for Fostering a Safety Culture

Several strategies can help healthcare organizations foster a culture of safety:

- Safety Training and Education: Providing regular training and education on patient safety, including simulation exercises, workshops, and e-learning modules.

- Implementing Safety Tools: Utilizing tools such as checklists, protocols, and safety bundles to standardize care and reduce variability.
- Promoting Teamwork: Encouraging teamwork through team-building activities, interdisciplinary rounds, and collaborative practice models.
- Enhancing Communication: Implementing communication tools such as SBAR, handoff checklists, and briefings to improve information exchange.
- Monitoring and Feedback: Regularly monitoring safety performance and providing feedback to staff. This includes safety audits, performance dashboards, and safety huddles.

The Role of Healthcare Providers

Healthcare providers are essential contributors to a culture of safety. They must be proactive in identifying and addressing safety issues, participate in safety initiatives, and collaborate with colleagues to enhance patient care. Providers should also engage in continuous learning and stay updated on best practices in patient safety.

Building a culture of safety is a collective effort that requires commitment and collaboration from all members of a healthcare organization. By prioritizing safety, fostering teamwork, and implementing effective strategies, healthcare providers can create a safe environment for patients.

MODULE THREE

LESSON ONE: EFFECTIVE COMMUNICATION IN HEALTHCARE

Communication is a critical component of patient safety, influencing every aspect of healthcare delivery. This lesson explores the importance of effective communication, common barriers, and strategies for improving communication in healthcare settings.

The Importance of Communication in Patient Safety

Effective communication is essential for ensuring safe and high-quality patient care. Miscommunication can lead to errors, misunderstandings, and adverse events. Clear and accurate communication among healthcare providers, as well as with patients and their families, is crucial for coordinating care and preventing harm.

Common Barriers to Effective Communication

Several barriers can hinder effective communication in healthcare:

- Hierarchical Structures: Traditional hierarchical structures can discourage open communication, particularly among junior staff members. Fear of speaking up and power dynamics can impede the flow of information.
- Workload and Time Pressures: High workload and time constraints can limit opportunities for thorough communication. Providers may rush through handoffs, consultations, and documentation, increasing the risk of errors.

- Language and Cultural Differences: Language barriers and cultural differences can lead to misunderstandings and misinterpretations. Effective communication requires sensitivity to diverse backgrounds and clear language.
- Technological Challenges: While technology can enhance communication, it can also create challenges. Issues such as electronic health record (EHR) usability, technical glitches, and information overload can affect communication.

Strategies for Improving Communication

Improving communication in healthcare requires a multifaceted approach. Key strategies include:

- Standardized Communication Tools: Utilizing standardized tools such as SBAR (Situation, Background, Assessment, and Recommendation), checklists, and handoff protocols can enhance communication clarity and consistency.
- Team Training: Providing training on communication skills and teamwork can improve collaboration and information exchange. Simulation training, workshops, and team-building activities are effective methods.
- Creating a Safe Environment: Encouraging a culture of openness and psychological safety where staff feel comfortable speaking up and sharing concerns without fear of reprisal.
- Technology Integration: Leveraging technology to facilitate communication, such as secure messaging systems, telemedicine, and decision support tools. Ensuring that technology is user-friendly and well-integrated into workflows.
- Patient and Family Engagement: Involving patients and their families in communication processes. This

includes using plain language, active listening, and confirming understanding through teach-back methods.

The Role of Healthcare Providers

Healthcare providers play a vital role in ensuring effective communication. They must actively engage in clear, concise, and accurate information exchange with colleagues, patients, and families. Providers should be mindful of potential barriers and take proactive steps to overcome them. Continuous improvement in communication skills is essential for enhancing patient safety.

Effective communication is a cornerstone of patient safety. By addressing common barriers and implementing strategies to enhance communication, healthcare providers can improve patient outcomes and reduce the risk of errors.

MODULE FOUR

LESSON ONE: STRATEGIES FOR INFECTION PREVENTION

Infection prevention is a critical aspect of patient safety, aimed at reducing the risk of healthcare-associated infections (HAIs). This lesson discusses the importance of infection prevention, key strategies, and best practices for healthcare providers.

The Impact of Healthcare-Associated Infections

Healthcare-associated infections (HAIs) are a significant concern in healthcare settings. They can lead to prolonged hospital stays, increased healthcare costs, and adverse patient outcomes. Common HAIs include catheter-associated urinary tract infections (CAUTIs), central line-associated bloodstream infections (CLABSIs), surgical site infections (SSIs), and ventilator-associated pneumonia (VAP).

Key Strategies for Infection Prevention

Effective infection prevention requires a combination of evidence-based strategies and best practices. Key strategies include:

- Hand Hygiene: Proper hand hygiene is the most effective way to prevent the spread of infections. Healthcare providers should follow hand hygiene guidelines, including washing hands with soap and water or using alcohol-based hand sanitizers.
- Environmental Cleaning: Regular cleaning and disinfection of healthcare environments, including patient rooms, operating rooms, and high-touch surfaces, are essential for preventing infections.

- Use of Personal Protective Equipment (PPE): Appropriate use of PPE, such as gloves, gowns, masks, and eye protection, helps to protect both healthcare providers and patients from infectious agents.
- Sterilization and Disinfection: Proper sterilization and disinfection of medical instruments and devices are critical for preventing infections. This includes following manufacturer guidelines and best practices for reprocessing equipment.
- Antimicrobial Stewardship: Promoting the appropriate use of antibiotics to prevent the development of antibiotic-resistant infections. This involves prescribing antibiotics only when necessary and selecting the appropriate antibiotic, dose, and duration.

Best Practices for Infection Prevention

Implementing best practices is essential for effective infection prevention. Key best practices include:

- Education and Training: Providing regular education and training on infection prevention practices for healthcare providers. This includes hands-on training, competency assessments, and updates on the latest guidelines.
- Surveillance and Monitoring: Conducting regular surveillance and monitoring of infection rates and trends. This involves collecting and analyzing data to identify areas for improvement and track the effectiveness of prevention efforts.
- Isolation Precautions: Implementing isolation precautions for patients with known or suspected infections. This includes using appropriate PPE, designating specific areas for isolation, and following protocols for the safe transfer of patients.

- Vaccination Programs: Promoting vaccination programs for healthcare providers and patients to prevent the spread of infectious diseases. This includes influenza vaccination, hepatitis B vaccination, and other relevant immunizations.
- Patient and Family Engagement: Educating patients and their families about infection prevention practices. This includes hand hygiene, respiratory etiquette, and adherence to isolation precautions.

The Role of Healthcare Providers

Healthcare providers play a crucial role in infection prevention. They must adhere to best practices, stay updated on guidelines, and participate in training and education programs. Providers should also engage in continuous improvement efforts and collaborate with colleagues to enhance infection prevention practices.

Infection prevention is a vital component of patient safety. By implementing evidence-based strategies and best practices, healthcare providers can reduce the risk of healthcare-associated infections and improve patient outcomes.

MODULE FIVE

LESSON ONE: MEDICATION SAFETY AND BEST PRACTICES

Medication safety is a critical aspect of patient safety, focused on preventing medication errors and adverse drug events (ADEs). This lesson discusses the importance of medication safety, common types of medication errors, and best practices for healthcare providers.

The Importance of Medication Safety

Medication errors can have serious consequences, leading to adverse drug events, patient harm, and increased healthcare costs. Ensuring medication safety involves accurate prescribing, dispensing, administration, and monitoring of medications. It also requires effective communication and patient education.

Common Types of Medication Errors

Understanding the common types of medication errors is essential for developing effective prevention strategies. Common types include:

- Prescribing Errors: Mistakes in the prescribing process, such as incorrect drug selection, dosage, route, or frequency. Prescribing errors can result from lack of knowledge, miscommunication, or incomplete patient information.
- Dispensing Errors: Errors that occur during the preparation and dispensing of medications. This includes incorrect labeling, wrong drug or dose dispensed, and errors in compounding medications.

- Administration Errors: Mistakes that occur during the administration of medications to patients. This includes administering the wrong dose, at the wrong time, via the wrong route, or to the wrong patient.
- Monitoring Errors: Failures to monitor the effects of medications appropriately. This can involve missing signs of adverse drug reactions, not conducting necessary lab tests, or failing to adjust dosages based on patient responses.

Best Practices for Medication Safety

Implementing best practices is crucial for ensuring medication safety. Key best practices include:

- Medication Reconciliation: Conducting thorough medication reconciliation during patient admissions, transfers, and discharges to ensure accurate and complete medication information.
- Standardized Protocols and Checklists: Using standardized protocols and checklists for prescribing, dispensing, and administering medications to reduce variability and errors.
- Barcode Medication Administration (BCMA): Utilizing barcode technology to verify patient identity and medication details before administration, ensuring accuracy.
- Computerized Physician Order Entry (CPOE): Implementing CPOE systems to reduce prescribing errors by providing clinical decision support and alerting providers to potential issues.
- Patient Education: Educating patients about their medications, including the correct dosages, potential side effects, and the importance of adherence to their prescribed regimens.

- Double-Check Systems: Implementing double-check systems, especially for high-risk medications, to ensure that two healthcare providers verify the medication details before administration.

The Role of Healthcare Providers

Healthcare providers play a critical role in ensuring medication safety. They must adhere to best practices, participate in continuous education and training, and engage in effective communication with colleagues and patients. Providers should also stay updated on the latest guidelines and advancements in medication safety.

Medication safety is an essential component of patient safety. By implementing best practices and fostering a culture of vigilance and continuous improvement, healthcare providers can significantly reduce the risk of medication errors and enhance patient outcomes.

CONCLUSION

Patient safety is a fundamental aspect of healthcare, directly impacting the quality of care and patient outcomes. As healthcare providers, our primary responsibility is to ensure that every patient receives safe, effective, and compassionate care. This book has outlined the essential principles, strategies, and practices necessary to achieve this goal.

Throughout the modules, we have explored various facets of patient safety, from understanding the nature and causes of medical errors to implementing robust safety cultures and effective communication strategies. Each lesson has provided practical guidance and evidence-based recommendations tailored to the unique challenges faced by healthcare providers.

Patient safety is a dynamic and ongoing effort that requires the commitment and collaboration of the entire healthcare team. By embracing the principles and strategies outlined in this book, healthcare providers can create safer environments and deliver the highest standard of care to their patients. Continuous education, vigilance, and a culture of safety will ensure that patient safety remains at the forefront of healthcare practice.

Let this book serve as a comprehensive resource and a call to action for all healthcare providers to prioritize patient safety in every aspect of their work. Together, we can make significant strides in reducing harm, improving outcomes, and enhancing the overall quality of care for patients.

REFERENCES

- Bates, D. W., & Gawande, A. A. (2003). *Improving safety with information technology. New England Journal of Medicine.*
- Berwick, D. M. (2003). *Disseminating innovations in health care.*
- Chassin, M. R., & Loeb, J. M. (2013). *High-reliability health care: Getting there from here. Milbank Quarterly.*
- Classen, D. C., Resar, R., Griffin, F., et al. (2011). *Global trigger tool shows that adverse events in hospitals may be ten times greater than previously measured. Health Affairs.*
- Donabedian, A. (2005). *Evaluating the quality of medical care. Milbank Quarterly.*
- Institute of Medicine. (1999). *To Err is Human: Building a Safer Health System. Washington, DC: National Academies Press.*
- Kohn, L. T., Corrigan, J. M., & Donaldson, M. S. (Eds.). (2000). *To Err is Human: Building a Safer Health System. Washington, DC: National Academies Press.*
- Leape, L. L., & Berwick, D. M. (2005). *Five years after To Err is Human: What have we learned?*
- Pronovost, P., Needham, D., Berenholtz, S., et al. (2006). *An intervention to decrease catheter-related bloodstream infections in the ICU. New England Journal of Medicine.*
- Reason, J. (2000). *Human error: Models and management.*
- Shojania, K. G., Duncan, B. W., McDonald, K. M., & Wachter, R. M. (Eds.). (2001). *Making Health Care*

Safer: A Critical Analysis of Patient Safety Practices. Agency for Healthcare Research and Quality.

- Vincent, C., & Amalberti, R. (2016). *Safer Healthcare: Strategies for the Real World. Springer International Publishing.*

www.ingramcontent.com/pod-product-compliance
Lightning Source LLC
Chambersburg PA
CBHW071259140726
47996CB00007B/2910

* 9 7 9 8 3 3 0 3 1 2 3 3 7 *